How to Write Poems

Joseph Coelho

ILLUSTRATED BY
Matt Robertson

BLOOMSBURY
Activity Books

Bloomsbury Children's Books
An imprint of Bloomsbury Publishing Plc

50 Bedford Square
London
WC1B 3DP
UK

1385 Broadway
New York
NY 10018
USA

www.bloomsbury.com

BLOOMSBURY and the Diana logo are trademarks of Bloomsbury Publishing Plc

First published in Great Britain 2017

ISBN: 9781408889497

2 4 6 8 10 9 7 5 3 1

Printed and bound in China by Leo Paper Products, Heshan, Guangdong

CONTENTS

CONTENTS

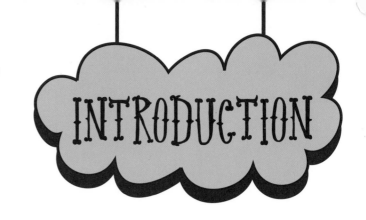

There is no secret to being a poet – anyone and everyone can be a poet! Writing is just one of the many tools that we use to express all the wonderful things going on in our heads.

In these pages you will learn that being brilliant at poetry is not all about writing. There is no right or wrong with poetry: the only rule is to have fun. So grab a pencil, a felt-tip or a crayon and write, draw and recite your way to a world of dazzling poems!

SILLY SIMILE ALERT

Watch out! Silly similes have escaped from my imagination, into this book. Can you spot them all?

Turn to page 44 to find out more.

YOU ARE A POET

First of all, let's warm up your imagination. Can you imagine yourself as a poet? What would you wear? Where would you write? Do you have a special notebook and pen? Use this space to draw yourself as a poet.

Where And When To Write

Here are some tips on how to get your poetic river flowing! Sometimes the hardest thing for a poet is finding the time and the space to write, so here are some tips to help you make a writing routine.

As soon as you wake up: jot down your first thoughts or record your dreams. If you start your day this way you will get into the habit of writing, so you're sure to create lots of fabulous poems!

Before you go to bed. Try thinking about everything you have seen or heard in the day – can you write a word, or a sentence, or a poem that sums up the day?

Where and when to write?

Whenever an idea hits: you never know when an idea might come to you so make sure you always have a notebook and a pen nearby. Write down a few words or do a doodle and label it – whatever will help you remember your great idea!

A quiet space. Maybe your teacher will let you use the reading corner during a break time, or perhaps there is a quiet spot in the lunch hall or a chair in the library. Having a quiet space means that you can collect your thoughts, and most importantly, listen out for all the great ideas that will be popping into your head.

On the move: make the most of your bus, train, or car journey to school. Get out your notebook and pen, look out of the window and write.

Can you add your own ideas?

Finding Inspiration

Inspiration and ideas can come from many places. Even overhearing people talking on a bus, or smelling something that jogs a memory – everyday events like this can be the starting point for a fantastic poem. Because ideas can come from anywhere, it is important to listen and to always remind yourself to hunt for poems around you.

Try hunting for poems by asking questions: what is that tree thinking? Where did that man get his hat from? Why did that smell make me sad? Look closely at the world around you and invite poetry ideas to come and settle inside your head! Use these pages to jot down some of those ideas.

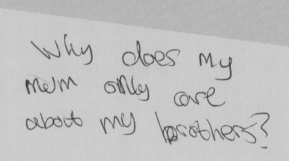

Why does my mum only care about my brothers?

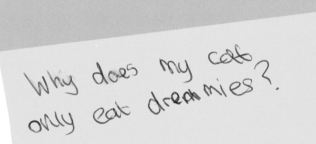

Why does my cat only eat dreamies?

11

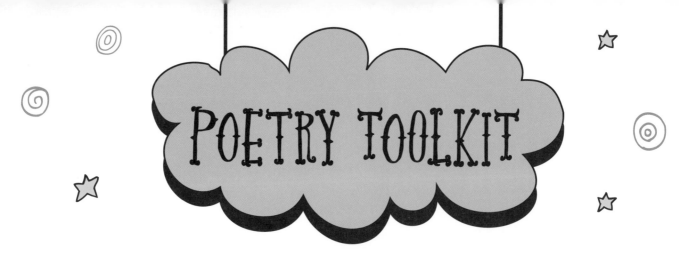

POETRY TOOLKIT

Now that you are a poet, you'll need a poetry toolkit to get you going! In this section you will find tips and tricks to make your poems sing.

Word Banks

Word banks are a collection of words: these words might become ideas for your poems. All you need is a pen and a piece of paper. Let's start with a theme, such as 'water'.

List all the words that you can think of that are associated (connected) with water. There are several ways to create a word bank: you could write your word bank as a spider diagram, a mind map, or a simple list.

Look at this list: can you add more words that are associated with water?

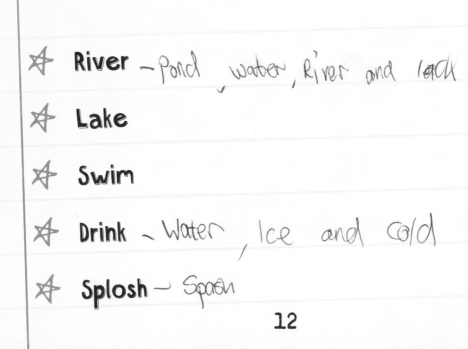

* **River** – Pond, water, River and lack

* **Lake**

* **Swim**

* **Drink** – Water, Ice and cold

* **Splosh** – Spash

12

However you collect your word bank, have fun finding the words – flick through books for inspiration and ask family and friends if they can think of any words related to your theme. You can keep adding to your word bank until you feel inspired enough to get writing!

Free Writing

Sometimes it's hard to think of ideas for poems. Sometimes you look at a blank sheet of paper and no ideas come, no matter how hard you screw up your face... chew your pencil... walk up and down... there are no ideas!

This is when free writing can help – write down whatever comes into your head even if the only thought is... "I DON'T KNOW WHAT TO WRITE". Even if you have to write this 100 times, just keep writing. You'll soon find that you are writing crazy words, silly words, serious sentences, funny sentences, and ideas will start to pop into your head. Magic!

I don't know what to write

I DON'T KNOW WHAT TO WRITE

oh, wait a minute...

I DON'T KNOW WHAT TO WRITE

YOU ARE A POET

How many words can you write in three minutes?

Time yourself writing whatever comes into your head for three minutes. Try to keep writing without stopping for the full time. When the time is up stop and count the words.

Write down how many words you counted here:

Can you beat your record? Have a competition with your friends.

I DON'T KNOW WHAT TO WRITE

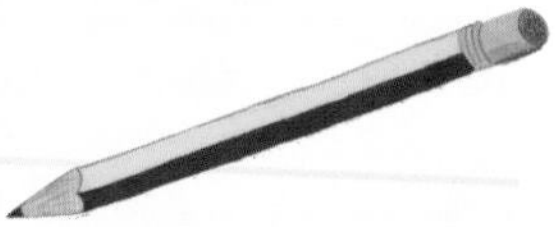

\#

♡
♡
♡

Now look at everything you have written down. Underline everything you like, even just one word, a sentence or an idea. Can you use any of the underlined bits in a new poem?

The "Make It Human" Personification Machine

Personification is a poetic tool which makes something that *isn't* human, sound a lot *more* human. Try using this personification machine: put an object in one end, turn the handle, and out pops the object from the other end – but this time it is more like a human . . .

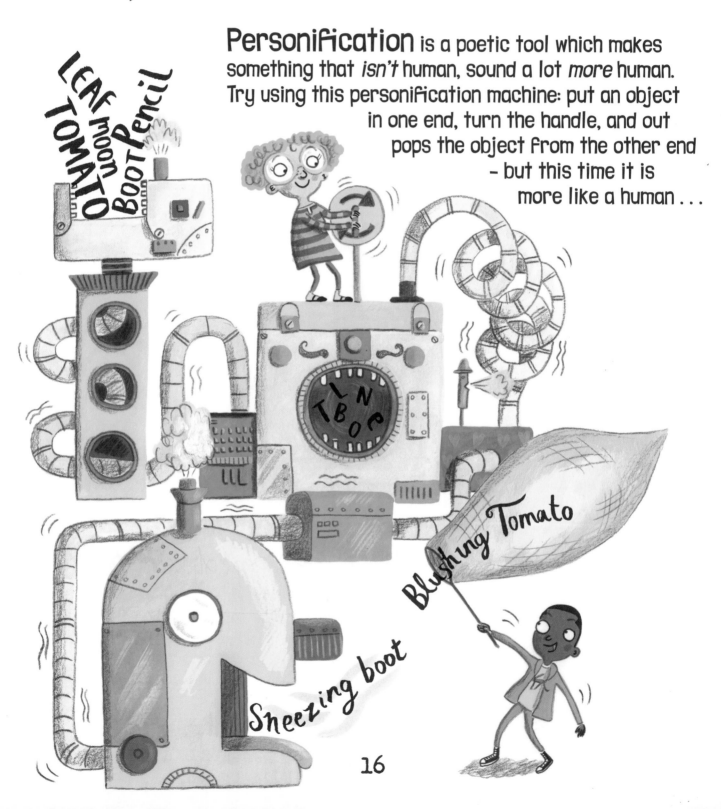

Let's put in
a TOMATO
Turn the handle . . .
And out pops . . .
A BLUSHING
TOMATO

Let's put in
something else,
like a BOOT
Turn the handle . . .
And out pops . . .
A SNEEZING BOOT

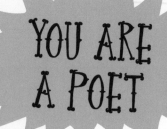

YOU ARE A POET

Make these things a little more human, how would they come out of the machine?

The moon	Turn the handle	all the way round and BOOM
A leaf	Turn the handle	and out poped a tree
A pencil	Turn the handle	
A dustbin	Turn the handle	

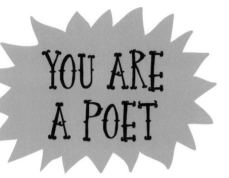

YOU ARE A POET

Try putting your new human-like objects into a sentence.
For example:

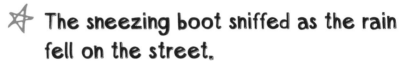
★ The sneezing boot sniffed as the rain fell on the street.

_____

_____

_____

_____

_____

_____

_____

_____

SILLY SIMILE ALERT

She had no energy, she felt like someone who had had a small breakfast.

Metaphor: the sun is an oven

With poems you can reimagine things, using poetic tools – like '**metaphor**': A metaphor is a way of reimagining something by saying that something IS something else. Metaphors make use of similarities between two very different things, to help us see those things in new ways. For example, this metaphor: 'the sun is an oven,' shows that both the sun and an oven are hot – this similarity means that the metaphor makes sense. Or you could say: 'the sun is a lightbulb', which makes sense because both the sun and a lightbulb give out light.

You can also create a metaphor by using language that is used to describe one thing, to describe something very different. For example: "the sun is **switched on** in the morning" takes the words you'd use to describe electric lights, but *instead* it uses them to describe the sun. Can you think of any more metaphors for the sun?

...switched on in the morning

YOU ARE A POET

You can even write an entire poem using metaphors! Try finishing the poem below: start each verse with one of the metaphors you created on page 20.

The sun is an oven
It bakes me on a hot summer's day
until my smiles rise like freshly baked bread.

The sun is a lightbulb
at night the light is switched off
and waits for morning to turn it on.

_____

_____

_____

_____

_____

_____

_____

_____

_____

_____

_____

_____

_____

_____

Senses

Using your senses in a poem can help bring it to life. This trick can make the difference between...

A roast chicken with potatoes and gravy.

and

A steaming, roasted, sizzling-in-the-oven chicken with hot, thick, meaty, bubbling gravy poured over crispy, warm-smelling potatoes.

What are your senses?

Smell – What you can smell with your nose.

Taste – What you can taste with your tongue.

Touch – What you can feel with your skin.

Sound – What you can hear with your ears.

Sight – What you can see with your eyes.

If you get stuck whilst writing, try to think about these five senses, to give you fresh inspiration. Start by describing where you are now, using only your senses...

What can you smell?

What can you taste?

What can you see?

What can you hear?

What can you feel?

Now you're thinking about your senses, it's easy to build up a poem on any theme you like. Take a look at the poem below and try writing your own!

Summer

I smell
the pollen of flowers blooming.
I taste
the green of grass in the air.
I see
the sun smiling brightly.
I hear
The swooping of the gulls.
I feel
The gentle breeze on my skin.

I smell flowers blooming in the sun bot while bees try to steal pollen

YOU ARE A POET

Abstract nouns are words that refer to feelings or concepts like hope, dreams, fear, confusion.

If you're looking for an extra challenge, try using your senses to describe an abstract noun. Pick an abstract noun and imagine what it would be like to smell it, taste it, see it, hear it and touch it. Would anger feel as hot as the sun? Would fear taste like crushed ice?

Write a poem about an abstract noun, but don't write down what the abstract noun is. Read the poem to a friend and see if they can guess which abstract noun you are talking about.

Here is an example, can you guess what it describes?

I smell like the promise of baked bread.
I am sweet and tasty on the tongue like a perfectly ripe apple.
I look like a rainbow – a sky palette of potential.
I sound like the rocking base line of a beat about to drop.
I feel soft like warm cat fur.
What am I?

Answer this way

27

The riddle on page 27 is written about an abstract noun, 'hope'.

A riddle is a poem which asks a question, (such as 'what am I?'), but doesn't give you an answer. Instead, it gives you clues so you can work out the answer! Try writing your own riddle using one of these abstract nouns: joy, dreams, courage, bravery, curiosity, determination, jealousy, trust. Ask a friend if they can guess what your riddle is about!

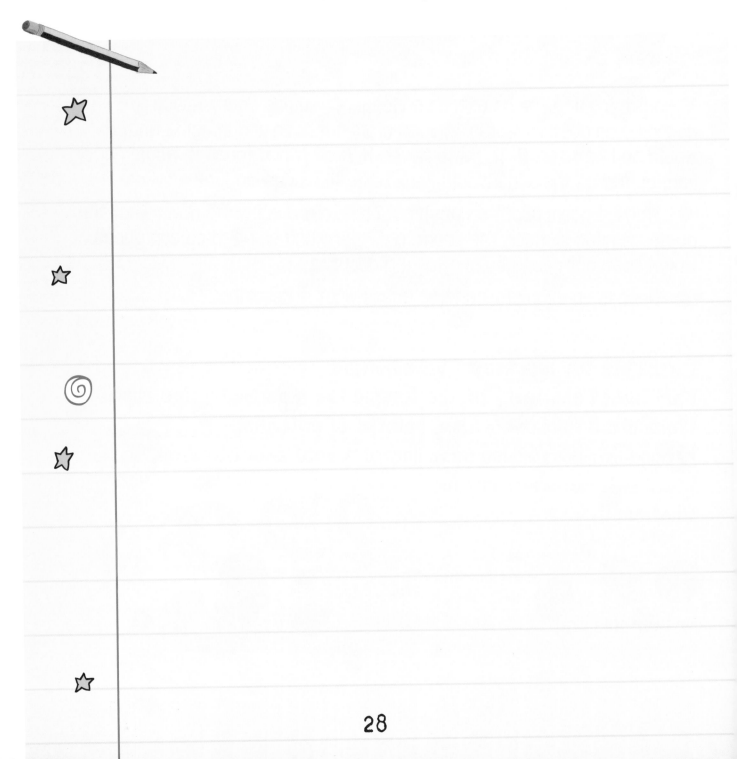

colours: rainbow thinking

When writing poems it can be fun to find new ways of describing things to make our writing even more exciting. So instead of calling something 'red', what if we said 'flaming lips', and instead of 'orange' we could say 'sun teardrops', and instead of 'green' we could say 'caterpillar skin'. These cool colour descriptions can be used in our poems, instead of the usual words for colours:

The fire engine screeched down the road in a blur of flaming lips racing through the sun-teardrop traffic lights and heading to the caterpillar-skin park.

Can you find new ways of describing these colours?
Try using these descriptions in your poems.

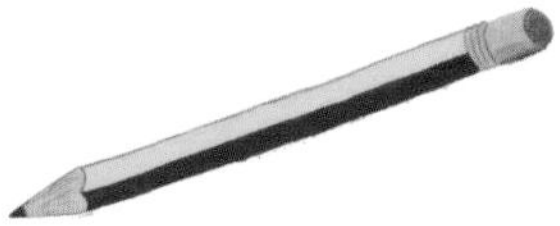

RED

YELLOW

PINK

GREEN

ORANGE

PURPLE

BLUE

GOLD   Bright

SILVER

BRONZE

GREY

WHITE plain white

BLACK

BROWN

Poetry Fact

Many paint companies give their paints more unusual names, such as:

Grey: Mole's Breath
Light brown: Wild Salmon
Pink: Cinder Rose

Next time you are in a shop that sells paint ask if you can have a colour chart - they are often given away for free and are filled with fantastic new names for colours.

RHYTHM AND RHYME: WORDS TO BE HEARD

In Ancient Greece, poets would recite poems whilst playing the lyre (an instrument that looks like a small harp, but is played like a guitar). When we recite poems nowadays, we don't always use music, but people still notice the rhythm and music of the poetry. Sometimes a beat can be heard in the way you recite your poem, and sometimes the type of words that you use can suggest music. Let's look at some tips for adding rhythm and musicality to your poetry.

Rap is short for 'rhythm and poetry' so all rappers are also poets!

Onomatopoeia: Banging, Crashing, Sizzling Poems!

Poems can bang
and poems can crash
poems can sizzle
kaboom and bash.

Poems can tinkle
and poems can ding
poems can grumble
and poems can ping.

Poems can bark
and poems can roar
poems can purr
and poems can snore.

Poets sometimes use sound words to include noises in their poems. These noises can give your poetry a rhythm. Sound words are also known as 'onomatopoeia', such as 'bang'. When you hit a drum you hear the sound 'bang' – but this is a word (as well as a sound). Another example is 'purr': when you stroke a cat you make it 'purr', but also the sound you hear is 'purr'. The sound makes a word. Whenever you use a sound that makes a word you are using onomatopoeia.

YOU ARE A POET

How many onomatopoeia (sound words) can you find in the poem above?

If you're looking for another challenge, try completing the poem below. Make sure you use lots of onomatopoeia!

Bang Went The Drums

Bang went the drums
Splash went the well
Boom went the clouds
and ring went the bells.

Roar went the ___Lion___
ding went the ___bells   on the___
___church doa___ went the _____
and ___swish went the wind___ went the _____

_____ went the _____
_____ went the _____
_____ went the _____
and _____ went the _____

Can you use onomatopoeia to write your own poem from scratch?

Alliteration:
Twisting The Tongue

This is the tale of terrible Tom
who had a tongue ever so long
that whenever he spoke
his tongue threatened to choke
his letters, his stories and songs.

Can you get your tongue around these tongue twisters?

"She sells sea shells on the sea shore."

"How much wood would a woodchuck chuck if a woodchuck could chuck wood."

Did you notice that a lot of these tongue twisters have words that start with the same letter? That's called 'alliteration'.

Poetry Fact

This tongue twister found by scientists
at The Massachusetts Institute
of Technology (MIT) is believed
to be one of the trickiest ever created.
See if you can manage it:

"PAD KID POURED CURD PULLED COD."

YOU ARE A POET

Build up a poem using your name, and lots of words that start with the same letter as your name:

Joe
Jumping Joe
Jumping Joe Juggles Jellyfish
Joyous Jumping Joe Juggles Jellyfish
Joyous Jumping Jogging Joe Juggles Jellyfish, Javelins and Jokes!

Now have a go at twisting your tongue around your own name – how long can you make your sentence?

In a house liges a mouse and the mouse likes to swish, bish, lish, dish and lives in the house that lish, swish, dish, bish in a house lives a mouse likes red lollys, yellow lollys, red lollys, yellow the lollys that he loves lives by the lake in the lovely water with the coool wind willows and that wen whish, whish whish but the Mouse likes to go lish, dish, swish, bish.

In A HOUSE lives a very naughty

MOUSE

38

Rhyme

Does poetry have to rhyme? Certainly not! But rhyming is fun – read on to make it easy...

Start by thinking of a word that you want to rhyme, for example 'night'. Now think of all the words that sound like 'night':

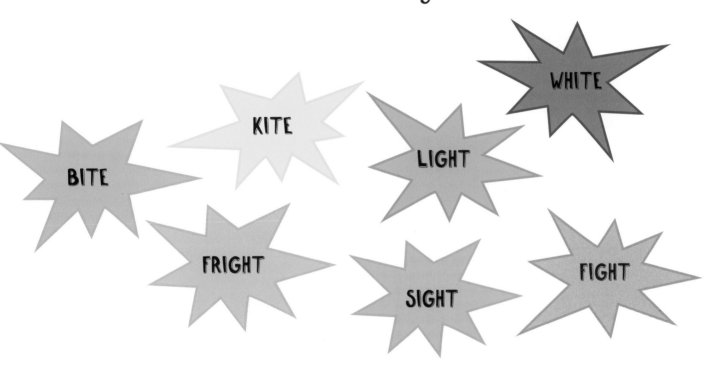

Now make sentences that end with those words...

_____

_____

_____

_____

_____

_____

_____

I'm a little vampire with a serious BITE
I transform into a bat and soar like a KITE
I strike fear with an almighty FRIGHT

Can you finish the poem above? Or write a new one from scratch, using the rhyming words on page 39.

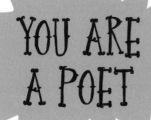

YOU ARE A POET

How about using two rhymes? It's not so tricky: just make two lists of rhyming words like this:

CHAIR
HAIR
CARE
BEAR
STARE
LAIR

SHAKE
BAKE
CAKE
SNAKE
LAKE
RAKE

Now create your sentences, but this time mix them up, like the example below... See what you can do with these rhyming endings, and don't worry about it making sense!

_____ CHAIR
_____ SHAKE
_____ HAIR
_____ BAKE
_____ CARE
_____ CAKE
_____ BEAR
_____ SNAKE
_____ STARE
_____ LAKE
_____ LAIR
_____ RAKE

SILLY SIMILE ALERT

His cheeks went as red as a baboon's bum.

Call And Response

"When I say 'pasta' you say 'cheese'... 'PASTA'"

"CHEESE"

"PASTA"

"CHEESE"

A poet might sometimes ask an audience to join in with a poem. Can you get an audience to join in this call and response?

Tell them what you will say (this is known as the 'call'). Write your 'call' below:

The call: When I say _____
(You could try using your favourite food like the example above).

Then tell them what they need to say in reply (this is known as the 'response'). Write the 'response' below.

The response: You say _____
(Choose a food that goes with the food in your 'call').

HIGH

LOW

Remember that you don't have to use food – you can use any two words that can be connected together – for example: high and low, summer and sun, vampire and bite.

YOU ARE A POET

This game will work with 2 people, or with 100! Ask everyone to stand in a circle. Take it in turns to shout out a call and response. For example, the first person will say "When I say 'pasta' you say 'cheese'". Everyone should then take part in the call and response four times.

The second person can then invent their own call and response. Keep playing around the circle: see how silly you can make the call and response. If someone can't think of one, or pauses for too long, or says the wrong response, then they are out!

Keep going until there are just two people left, then try and do the call and responses as quickly as possible until you have a winner.

SILLY SIMILE ALERT

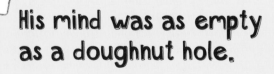

His mind was as empty as a doughnut hole.

Similes

A simile uses "as" and "like" to compare two things, for instance:

"The monster's skin was **like** wet leaves."

"The alien's breath smelled as rotten **as** a three-year-old cabbage."

Similes help us to describe things that other people may not have seen or experienced, by making a comparison with something they will have seen or experienced. Not many people have seen a purple monster with crazy hair, but if you say that its hair is **like** candyfloss or **as** sticky as candyfloss, people will know what the monster's hair is like! Similes help us to make the imagined more real.

Unfortunately, several silly similes have escaped into the rest of this book. Can you find them?

SILLY SIMILE ALERT

His shout was as high-pitched as a skyscraper.

44

YOU ARE A POET

Grab a pen and some sticky notes, you're about to go on a simile hunt! Make sure you check with an adult first, then step outside and search for similes. Look in your playground at school, in your local park, in your garden. Look at all the different colours and textures around you, what do they remind you of?

A green blade of grass might make you think of the colour of a monster's back. Write the simile on a sticky note: "The monster's back was as green as grass", and stick it ON the blade of grass.

The texture of a brick wall might make you think of the texture of an alien's face. Write the simile on a sticky note: "The alien's face was rough, hard and flakey like an old brick wall", and stick this on the wall itself!

Keep looking for different similes – what do the colours of the leaves remind you of? And the glint of a spider's web? See if you can find ten or more similes. Then collect up all of your sticky notes and place them on pages 46 and 47. You now have a bank of simile ideas that you can use in your poems.

Collect your simile hunt sticky notes on these pages!

FABULOUS FORM

Poetry can take many forms: it can be long or short, it can be shaped and written to a rule, or have no rules at all. Many of the forms have names: there are sonnets and funny limericks, snappy haikus, splendid shape poems and crazy clerihews. On these next few pages you can fill in the gaps to complete the different types of poem, to get people laughing and gasping at your poetic prowess!

Syllables: How Many Sounds In A Word?

Every word can be broken up into a group of sounds called syllables. The word WATER has two syllables: 'WA' and 'TER'. There is an easy trick to figure out how many sounds are in a word: put your hand close under your chin, leaving a 1cm gap between them. Now say the word 'water', and count how many times your chin touches your hand. This should happen twice: once when you say 'wa', and again when you say 'ter'. Each time your chin touches your hand, that's a syllable. Can you count the number of syllables in these words...

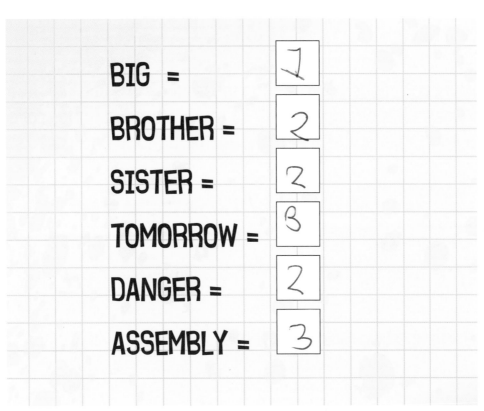

BIG = 1

BROTHER = 2

SISTER = 2

TOMORROW = 3

DANGER = 2

ASSEMBLY = 3

Some poetic forms have a set number of syllables, to create a specific rhythm and structure. Writing these poems is easy, just remember to put your hand under your chin and keep trying different sentences - until you find one that has all the syllables you need.

Haikus

A haiku is a famous form of Japanese poetry. Each one is just three lines long! Sounds easy? To make things a little more challenging, there are a set number of syllables in each line.

Line 1 has **five** syllables: Green leaves on the trees

Line 2 has **seven** syllables: Rustle in the springtime wind

Line 3 has **five** syllables: I smell the flowers.

So the whole haiku looks like this:

> **Green leaves on the trees**
> **Rustle in the springtime wind**
> **I smell the flowers.**

YOU ARE
A POET

Have a go at writing a haiku. Remember to put your hand under your chin to count the syllables! It might not be easy first time: try changing some words or swapping words around to get the correct number of syllables on each line.

Super Simple One-Word Poems

Poems can be as long or as short as you like: the idea behind the poem is what is important! Some poets have found a clever way to create one-word poems... they make the title quite long:

The Sad Tale Of A Fly

SPLATT!

Can you write a one-word poem, like the poem above? Think of the title as the set-up, or framing, for your one word. Choose a topic and see where your imagination takes you.

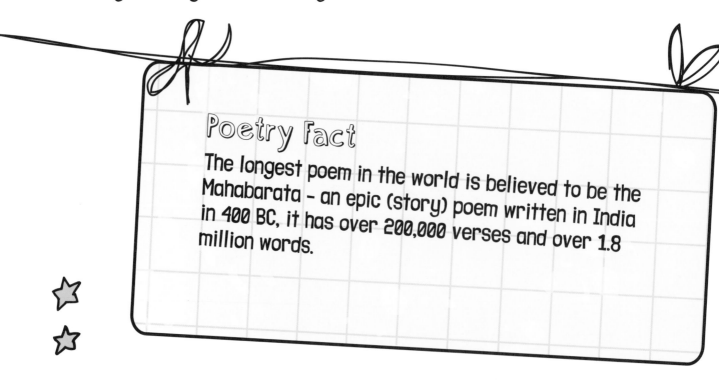

Poetry Fact
The longest poem in the world is believed to be the Mahabarata - an epic (story) poem written in India in 400 BC, it has over 200,000 verses and over 1.8 million words.

Acrostics: Vertical-Side Poems

Acrostics are poems that use one super special word to inspire all the other words to come. First of all, you need a word that you want to write about. Let's take the word SUN and write it down the side of the page like this:

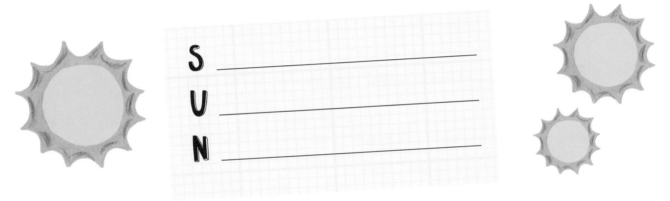

Now think of a sentence about the sun that starts with each letter, like this:

Summer's mask has a smiling heat.
Umbrella hating this golden disk,
Never comes out in the rain.

The longer the word you start with, the longer your poem will be!

YOU ARE A POET

Use the name of a friend to write an acrostic poem. Think of all the things you like about them, and then give them the poem as a gift.

Abecedarius: Amazing Alphabet Poems

An alphabet poem has a simple flow

Because each line starts with a letter you know

Children can master them, adults can too

Dinosaurs can have a go but . . .

Emus haven't a clue.

First write out the alphabet from A–Z

Give each letter a sentence (it's so easy)

However as you get nearer to the bottom

It can get tricky to stop the poem going rotten

Just have fun, that's the

Key to this one

Let the words flow, let the

Monkey go!

Never mind the monkey! How did he get here?

Obviously this poem is

Pulling your ear!

Quarrelsome poem!

Remember that each line does not have to follow

what's just been

Some poets have fun by exploring a

Theme . . .

Umbrellas are personal trees,

Very good at keeping us dry.

Wet weather can't play your

Xylophone bones with its tinkle when

Your umbrella protects you from the rain's

Zapping downpour.

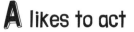

YOU ARE A POET

In case you didn't notice, an abecedarius poem is based on the order of the alphabet! They can be written on any theme: the poem below is based on the possible 'characters' of each letter in the alphabet. Can you finish it off?

A likes to act

B is a brave chancer

C is great at crying

D is a hip hop dancer

E _____

F _____

G _____

H _____

I _____

J _____

K _____

L _____

M _____

N _____

O _____

P _____

Q _____

R _____

S _____

T _____

U _____

V _____

W _____

X _____

Y _____

Z _____

SILLY
SIMILE
ALERT

She yawned like a
burping frog.

Mesostic: Vertical-Middle Poems

These poems look like a spine, with a sentence for each rib. Just like an acrostic poem, a mesostic poem has one word running vertically through the poem. However, with a mesostic poem, that word runs down the middle (rather than at the start) of each line. Here is an example, can you see the hidden word?

when I get very sad, i**T** kicks off as a prickling,

a bubbling trailing my **E**yes, popping, fizzing

rushing to drown **A**ll of my attempts

to look no**R**mal and happy

just like **S**omeone who never cries.

YOU ARE
A POET

Create your own mesostic using the word LAUGH. Think of the last time you couldn't stop laughing: how did it feel? What was your body doing? Who was with you? What made you giggle? Can you create mesostics for the other words on this page?

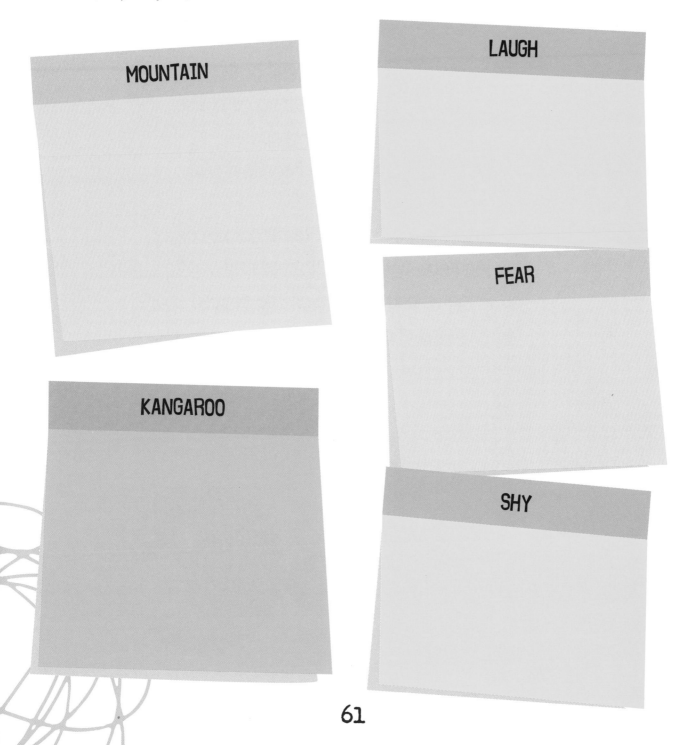

MOUNTAIN

LAUGH

FEAR

KANGAROO

SHY

Simple Sonnets

There is a monster that lurks in the sea
he has a problem you never could guess,
a problem that is hard to conceive
he has grown far too big for his dress.

His skirts are much smaller than before
his leggings, are much tighter still
he wriggles and writhes on the seabed shore
he's tugging and pulling with all of his skill.

He misses the tassels of his flowery robe
and the pink of his ripped-denim Levi's
he needs a brand new monster wardrobe
but none of the shops do monster size.

Many at sea have had a great big scare
of a humongous monster with nothing to wear.

If you love rhyme, sonnets are the poetic form for you! A sonnet is 14 lines of rhyming poetry. Each sonnet is made up of four verses, and each verse has lines that rhyme. Below are some rhyming words to get you going: can you fill in the blanks?

The first verse has four lines:

1 _____ light

2 _____ stare

3 _____ bright

4 _____ care

Notice how the 1st line rhymes with the 3rd line, and the 2nd line rhymes with the 4th line.

The second verse also has four lines:

5 _____ tree

6 _____ head

7 _____ me

8 _____ bed

Notice how the 5th line rhymes with the 7th line and the 6th line rhymes with the 8th line.

The third verse has four lines as well:

⑨ _____ pop

⑩ _____ bang

⑪ _____ hop

⑫ _____ fang

Notice how the 9th line rhymes with the 11th line and the 10th line rhymes with the 12th line.

The fourth verse has only two lines, which rhyme with each other:

⑬ _____ treat

⑭ _____ complete

Poetry Fact:

William Shakespeare wrote at least 154 sonnets, many of these were about love.

Clerihews

A clerihew is a simple four-line poem about someone famous. A clerihew rhymes and is often funny: this is a chance to make your audience laugh! Let's start off with a clerihew about a superhero.

The first line is a superhero's name

The third line tells us a bit more about the person

The Incredible Hulk
is a great green bulk
who grows muscles when he is mad.
His muscles rip his trousers, this makes him very sad.

The second line rhymes with the superhero's name

The fourth line rhymes with the third line and has a funny ending

YOU ARE A POET

A good starting place when writing your clerihew is to think of some words that rhyme with the name of the person (or superhero) you are writing about:

Thor rhymes with: bore, door, coleslaw

Hercules rhymes with: fleas, bees, knees

Wolverine rhymes with: mean, machine, bean, green

Storm rhymes with: warm, swarm, reform

Write a clerihew about one of the superheroes on page 66, or a famous person you like.

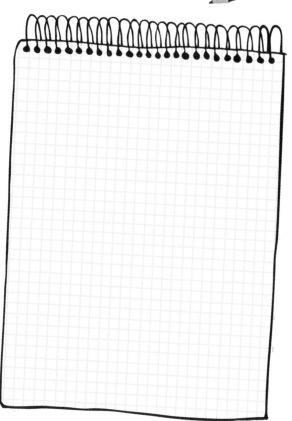

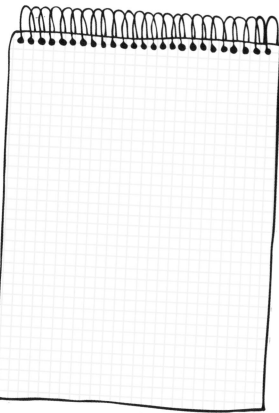

Found Poems

Have you ever found an accidental poem? Maybe you overheard a bit of a conversation and it sounded like a poem. Or maybe you've glanced down the spines of some books, or DVDs on a shelf, and the titles have made a poem.

Found poems are poems that have accidentally formed – and you have been lucky enough to find them! You can spot a found poem wherever there are words: in a recipe book, inside a computer game, on an instruction manual.

YOU ARE A POET

Can you spot a 'found poem'? You could look inside a newspaper or magazine, or the contents pages of a book or the weather reports on the radio – hunt for words and phrases that you think sound beautiful. Write your poem on page 69:

Shape Poetry

Shape poetry takes the shape of something connected to the poem. This is only limited by your imagination! You might write a poem about a bike, and shape the poem to look like a bike. Or you could write a poem *about* a pyramid and *shape* it like a pyramid, like this:

Beneath
this monument of
empires faded. Lies the husks
of royalty jaded. Preserved and
wrapped in their mummy bed they
hope to be whisked to the land of the dead.

You can also make a sentence of a poem follow the line of a shape you draw like this:

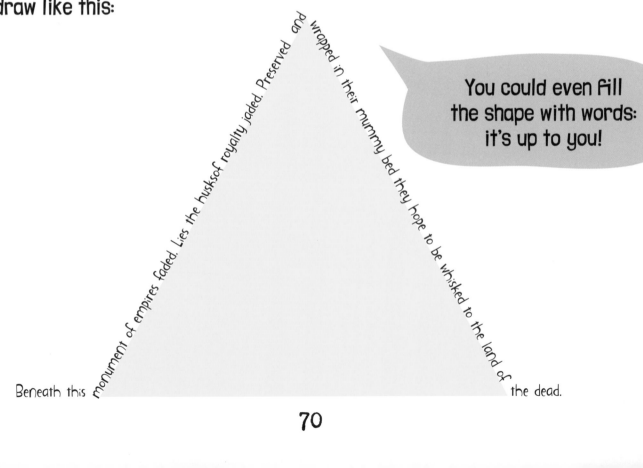

You could even fill the shape with words: it's up to you!

YOU ARE A POET

Making shape poetry is easy, you just need to fit your line breaks into the shape. Test this out on the shapes below. Start with a pencil – it can be tricky to make all the words fit, but you can always change words, add words, or leave some words out. Experiment with writing around the shape, or writing inside the shape, or try writing in different font styles or colours. There is no limit to the different styles and techniques – see how creative you can be!

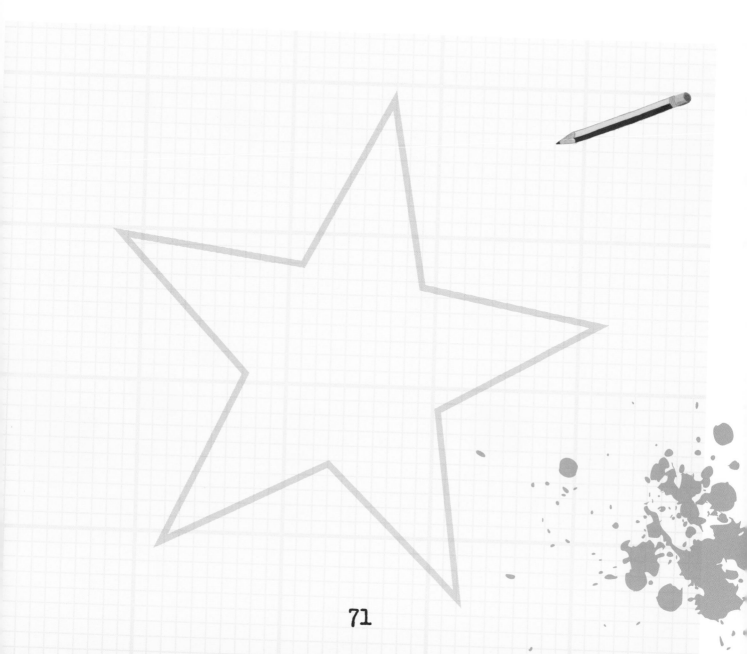

74

Photo Poetry

There is another brilliant technique for making your own picture poem... you can use a photo! Collect together the following:

 A photograph that you like (a large photo works best because it gives you lots of space to work with – you can ask an adult to use a photocopier to make your photograph bigger)

 Some tracing paper

 A pencil

 A rubber

 Colouring pencils

 Paperclips

Place the tracing paper on top of the photograph and secure with the paperclips. Using your pencil, start to write your poem on the tracing paper, following the outlines of the photograph. Don't be afraid to rub out mistakes, and lift up the tracing paper every now and again to see how your picture poem is looking. When you have finished, your poem should look like the photograph! Now grab your colouring pencils and go over the pencil words.

YOU ARE A POET

Photocopy a photo of yourself and use this to make an autobiographical photo poem. Write a poem all about yourself! You could write about the things you are proud of, your hopes for the future, your friends and family – it's up to you! Stick your poem in the frame on the next page.

Blackout Poems

Now you're ready for a challenge! A blackout poem is a bit like a found poem, because you need to start with some old text that nobody wants: it might be a flyer from a show, a page from a newspaper or magazine, or even some junk mail. Grab a felt-tip (works best if it's a dark colour) and simply black out any words you don't want, so you're left with only the words of your poem. Slowly build up the poem like this. You can even black out parts of a word to reveal words hiding inside.

The example below is created from an old instruction manual. In those instructions the word WITCH was hiding inside the word SWITCH, which inspired a poem about a witch!

Remove the
lights
in the
clock remove the clock
turn ON TIME
witch
One
lights
The hours, of
the following day.
Switching off
cutting
the war
rat
This
animal
This rat
ensuring the weather
must be disposed of accordingly
becomes damaged
light
The heat
near any
is
rage.

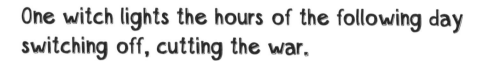

You can choose to write out your poem afterwards - you could add punctuation or play around with the words given to you from the blackout poem. Here is the poem opposite typed out:

Light the Hours

"Remove the lights in the clock
remove the clock, turn on TIME."

One witch lights the hours of the following day
switching off, cutting the war.

"This rat animal,
this rat, ensuring the weather becomes damaged
must be disposed of accordingly.
the lights near any heat rage."

Using quotation marks creates the feeling of the witch talking to us.

YOU ARE A POET

Have fun searching for poems by "blacking out" words and try experimenting with different colour felt-tips. Poetry really is everywhere, it's just waiting to be discovered!

FUNNY POEMS

Your challenge in this chapter: to make your audience laugh! Poetry can be very funny, but it can be tricky to write funny poems. Over the next few pages we'll look at some tips and tricks to make you a hilarious poet...

Laughing Limericks

Some forms of poems are particularly good at being funny. First up: the limerick! Limericks tell a funny story about someone from a particular place. The first line introduces the place, then the rest of the lines tell us something funny about the person. Limericks have five lines, and lines one, two and five rhyme with each other. For example:

These lines rhyme with each other

1. There was a young man from Southsea
2. Who drank gallons of weak tea.
3. He drank straight from the pot
4. He drank it ice-cold and hot
5. and constantly needed to pee.

These lines have a different rhyme

To start off, think of a place to set your limerick. Now find some words that rhyme with that place and create a rhyme list.

Rhyme list for 'Southsea'

Me	Bee
Tea	She
Pee	He
Free	

Now choose the words from your rhyme list that have some sort of connection – this might give you an idea for the rest of the poem.

Before you get going, think about the syllables in your limerick. Lines one, two and five are the longest lines in a limerick. There are normally seven to ten syllables in these lines. (Remember to use the counting syllables trick from page 48!)

You might have noticed that lines three and four also rhyme with each other: 'pot' and 'hot' in the limerick opposite. These lines are the shortest – they are normally five to seven syllables long.

YOU ARE A POET

Now have a go at creating your own limerick. Can you fill in the limericks below?

1 There was a young man from New York

2 _____ pork

3 _____

4 _____

5 _____ fork

How about this one?

Cross out the word you don't want to use

1 _____ Mars

2 _____ bras or cars or stars

3 _____

4 _____

5 _____ bras or cars or stars

82

Or this rhyme about Putney, in London.

1 ——————————————————— Putney

2 ——————————————————— chutney or gluttony

3 ———————————————————

4 ———————————————————

5 ——————————————————— chutney or gluttony

Now try writing some limericks from scratch! Remember, start off with a place name, then create a rhyme list and use this to find some words that connect with the place name.

SILLY SIMILE ALERT

The sun was like a bowl of custard.

Nonsense Poems

Nonsense poems can seem like just that - nonsense! When you first read them they might not make sense, but if you keep reading them you might find they do make sense in a weird way: it's like the poet is creating a new world.

Here's a fantastic way to write nonsense poems: write about something ordinary and then swap in some nonsense words, like this...

Here's a poem about going to assembly:

The bell rings

our (teacher) asks us students to line up by the door

we walk quietly to the assembly hall

our (teacher) asks us to sit in a straight line

other lines of students walk in and sit behind us

their (teachers) tell them to be quiet

Our head (teacher) tells us many things until the bell rings.

Notice that some words are repeated

84

Now choose some words from your ordinary poem and swap them with funny or made-up words. Make sure you swap some of the words you repeated in the ordinary poem!

The Swap List

Teacher = Flambgizzle

Bell = Grumptank

Line = Crocaduck

Students = Slimfry

Door = Swing-a-och

Quiet = Shushbee

Walk = Swagglebum

Assembly = Moot

Sit = Butterdom

If we swap these words into our poem, we'll end up with:

The grumptank rings
our flambgizzle asks us slimfry to crocaduck up by the swing-a-och
we swagglebum shushbeely to the moot hall
our flambgizzle asks us to butterdom in a straight crocaduck
other crocaducks of slimfry swagglebum in and butterdom behind us
their flambgizzles tell them to be shushbee
Our head flambgizzle tells us many things
until the grumptank rings.

It's important to repeat some of the words: as the audience will hear them more than once, they'll get a hint at what they might mean, and so the poem will kind of make sense – in a nonsense poem kind of way!

Here's another ordinary poem about eating an orange:

I pick up a plump ripe round orange,
it makes my mouth drool,
it smells delicious and orangey.
I stick my nail into the orange's firm skin
and start to peel, digging my nails in.
The orange juice stains the skin of my fingers.
I peel all of the skin off.
The orange segments are plump and ripe.
I bite into its flesh and feel its juice roll around my mouth.

Complete this swap list with your own made-up words:

Plump = _____

Ripe = _____

Orange = _____

Mouth = _____

Nail = _____

Skin = _____

Juice = _____

Peel = _____

Fingers = _____

Bite = _____

Now fill in the gaps with the made-up words from your list!

I pick up a _____ _____ round _____,
it makes my _____ drool,
it smells delicious and _____ey.
I stick my _____ into the _____'s firm
_____
and start to _____, digging my _____s in.
The _____ _____ stains the _____
of my _____.
I _____ all of the _____ off.
The _____ segments are _____ and _____.
I _____ into its flesh and feel its _____ roll
around my _____.

YOU ARE A POET

Ask a group of friends to join you in writing some short poems about very ordinary things – like going to the shops or waiting for a bus. Make sure that they repeat some words in their poems.

When everyone has finished writing, swap the poems around. Using the poem that you have been given, make a swap list of made-up words (like the one opposite).

Once you have each got a swap list, rewrite your friends' poem with the new made-up words in place. Whose is the funniest?

Turn over for extra writing space!

_____

_____

_____

_____

_____

_____

_____

_____

_____

_____

_____

_____

Sometimes putting bits of other words together can inspire made-up words, like 'CROCADUCK', (crocodile and duck).

AWESOME ADVENTURE AND ACTION POEMS

I'm swinging from a giant's moustache
I'm sprinting down a dragon's back
I'm crouching under a tiger's belly
I don't want to be a monster's snack!

Adventures get the heart racing and the blood pumping!
They are fun to read and even better to write.
To create an awesome adventure poem you'll need:
a brilliant setting, an inspiring hero,
a terrifying baddie, and some exciting
action words.

The Beginnings of An Adventure

Settings:

A setting is where a story or a poem takes place. An adventure could take place anywhere: on another planet, inside a teapot, in a jungle, in a deep dark wood, under the sea – your imagination is the limit!

Heroes:

Great adventures also have inspiring heroes: perhaps a warrior princess, a skateboarding prince, a motorbike-riding queen, a ballerina king?

Baddies:

No adventure is complete without some terrifying baddies: a thieving ogre, a spiteful dragon, a thundering troll, a mean giant, a loathsome monster – or something completely different!

Scribble some ideas for different settings, heroes and baddies, to inspire an EPIC adventure poem. Use these tips to help you write your adventure poem the way you want, remember there is no right or wrong.

SETTINGS

HEROES

BADDIES

Climbing, Running, Leaping: Adventure Verbs

Adventures need: a brilliant setting, an inspiring hero, and a terrifying baddie. They also need some action!

Action words (verbs) bring a poem to life. They help us imagine what is happening in the adventure and make us feel that we are taking part. Action words often end with "ing".

Next time you are in the playground think about all of the different actions you are using:

Climbing up a climbing frame
Spinning on a roundabout
Swinging from a rope
Jumping into puddles

Imagine that instead of doing all of those things in a park or playground, you are doing them in a fantastic, magical setting:

Climbing up a martian mountain

Spinning in a crashing spaceship

Swinging from a jungle vine

Jumping into a monster's mouth

This sounds like the beginning of an awesome adventure poem!

YOU ARE A POET

Can you add some action words (verbs) to the space below?

Skulking

Running

Galloping

Hopping

Sprinting

Sliding

Tip-toeing

Sneaking

Use your action words and the settings, heroes, and baddies on pages 94 and 95 to inspire your very own adventure poem!

SILLY SIMILE ALERT

Her tears fell like water dripping from a tap that had not been turned off **properly**.

YOU ARE A POET

Get ready for an imaginary adventure! This game is great to play on a climbing frame – in a park, or at school in the playground.

Gather 2-15 people. Choose one person to be the caller. As everyone else slides, swings, climbs and runs the caller waits and then without warning shouts **"FREEZE!"**

Everyone must stop what they are doing. The caller will then point at someone and ask them to shout out what they are doing. Sounds easy, but this is where your imagination comes in! You must describe what you are doing as though you're in an adventure poem – so if you are sliding down a slide, imagine that the slide is something else and say something like: "I am sliding down a giant's tongue!"

FREEZE!
What's happening on your adventure?

If you are climbing a ladder, imagine you are climbing something else and say something like: "I am climbing up a giant beanstalk!"

The caller must ask everyone at least once - if someone cannot answer, or takes too long to answer, then they become the caller. The original caller can play with the others until they hear - "FREEZE!"

If everyone manages to imagine something the caller shouts out "UNFREEZE" and the game continues.

NATURE POEMS

Nature is everywhere: even in the most built up city centre you can spot plants sprouting in the cracks of the pavements, little flowers growing between bricks, leaves blowing on the wind, birds flying in the sky, clouds making different shapes, the sun blazing down, rain falling, insects buzzing. All these things might inspire you to write poetry!

YOU ARE A POET

Find a big leaf. Look at the different colours in the leaf, is it green? If so, what kind of green? Look closer - are there other colours at the edges, or near the stem? Smell the leaf, what does it smell like? What shape is the leaf?

Use a dark felt-tip pen (with a thin nib) to write down your thoughts about the leaf - on the leaf itself. You can also write lots of words on many leaves. When you have finished writing, collect all your leaves and stick them together, on the next pages, to create a poem made out of leaves.

Turn over for extra
writing space!

Poetry Fact

The 'Poem Tree' in Wittenham Clumps (Oxfordshire) is a dead beech tree that has a whole poem carved into its bark. The poem was carved by Joseph Tubb in 1844 and is inspired by his love of the landscape. (Do not try this! Trees are very sensitive and if you carve their bark they can die. Stick to writing on leaves instead.)

Water

The Ancient Greeks believed that nature was made up of elements, including: earth, water, air, fire. Thinking about nature in this way might inspire some poetry...

Water

Rolling down a waterfall
after a trip down a lazy river
falling into an ice cold pond
your body all a shiver.

Water: we drink it, bathe in it, shower in it, swim in it and play in the rain. It is essential to our survival. A water-themed poem could be about many different things:

★ A pond that you know and the wildlife within it
★ Going swimming
★ Brushing your teeth
★ How it feels to drink your favourite drink
★ A trip you took on a boat
★ Getting caught in the rain

Can you solve this riddle?

What has a bed but never sleeps,
has a mouth but never eats,
has a bank but no money?

ANSWER: A RIVER

YOU ARE A POET

Remember the 'make it human' personification machine on page 16? Try using personification to write a poem from the point of view of a river. Imagine that a river is alive...

How old is the river?

Is the river male or female?

How does he or she feel?

What is his/her name?

Where does he/she travel to and from?

You could use onomatopoeia (turn to page 33), such as drip, splish, crash, gurgle, roar. Think about this river as though it is a person and use your poem to tell their story!

Earth

The Earth Giant

His eyes glint like the blackest Obsidian rocks,
his mouth is filled with Quartz crystals,
his temper flares like a lava shock,
his shout is like a firing pistol.

Let the earth inspire you! Think about some 'earthy' words, such as:

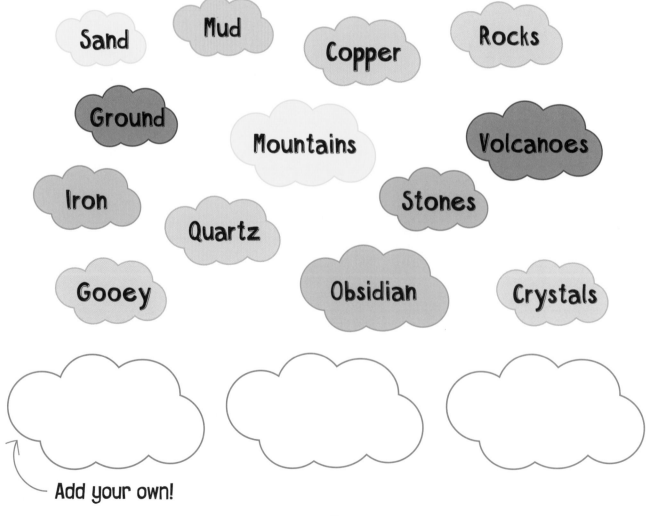

Sand

Mud

Copper

Rocks

Ground

Mountains

Volcanoes

Iron

Stones

Quartz

Gooey

Obsidian

Crystals

Add your own!

Can you use some of these words to finish off *The Earth Giant* poem opposite? You could write about his hands and arms, where he lives, what has made him so angry... or anything else!

If you want an extra challenge, see if you can make the lines rhyme like in the first verse: the 1st and 3rd line rhyme, and the 2nd and 4th line have a different rhyme.

Turn over for extra writing space!

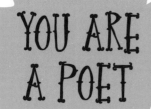

YOU ARE A POET

Use the earth itself to write a GIANT poem. You will need:

⭐ A sturdy stick
⭐ A place with muddy, earthy ground or a sandy beach (if you don't have either of these, but you do have some pebbles, turn to the next 'You Are a Poet' challenge!)

Use the stick to write a poem in the mud or the sand. Is your poem inspired by the earth itself? Try making the letters different sizes.

His voice was like a zip on a broken pencil case.

SILLY SIMILE ALERT

YOU ARE A POET

Try making a poem out of pebbles! Gather lots of smooth pebbles, about the size of your palm. Grab a permanent marker and write your poem one word at a time - a word on each pebble. Lay the pebbles out in front of you to make sentences. Try rearranging the pebbles to create new poems, or drop them into a bag, wiggle them around, and drop them out to create random sentences. You could take a photo of any poems you like and stick them on these pages!

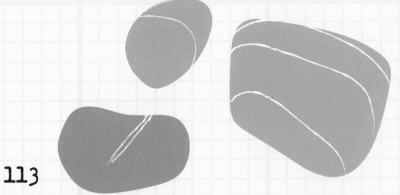

Fire

Fire can be a useful thing: we use it to cook our food, heat our homes and light our candles, but it can also be very destructive and deadly. This could inspire you to write a poem in three stages:

A Chicken

A chicken.
Cold, pink and raw,
skin like my grandmother's hands.

Cook

A roast chicken.
Its smell making my belly rumble,
sitting in gravy with egg-like potatoes.

Burn

A burnt chicken.
A blackened carcass,
smoke filling the kitchen my eyes tearing.

This poem describes a chicken before being cooked, after being cooked and after being burnt.

You can use this idea for anything, such as a candle:

Verse 1 – Before being lit: the room is dark, the candle whole.

Verse 2 – After being lit: the candle melts, the room is bright.

Verse 3 – The candle is all used up, the room is dark.

Or a plant:

Verse 1 – A seed in the ground.

Verse 2 – Sunlight warms the soil, the seed grows.

Verse 3 – The sun gets too hot, the plant wilts.

Can you write a poem in three verses, inspired by the examples above?

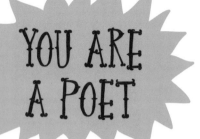

YOU ARE A POET

You are going to write an invisible poem! Collect together the following:

- ✦ **An old white candle or a white crayon**
- ✦ **A large piece of paper or card**
- ✦ **Paint or a thick felt-tip pen**
- ✦ **A paintbrush**

Hold the candle like a pen and write on the paper or card. (It is best to use the edge of the candle for writing.) The wax will leave an almost invisible trail of words.

When you have finished writing, paint or scribble with the thick felt-tip over the poem to reveal the words, like magic! If you want to impress a friend or family member, you could write them a secret poem, and give them instructions on how to reveal the poem later, using paint or a felt-tip.

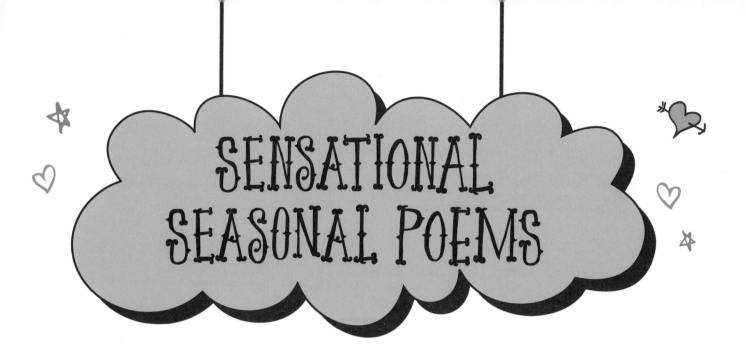

SENSATIONAL SEASONAL POEMS

Exciting occasions in the calendar year could also get you scribbling!
Let's look at a few special occasions, and the poems they might lead to.

Mother's Day and Father's Day

Once every year you get to tell your mum, dad or carer just how special
they are. You could write a poem to say thank you for all that they do.
Here's a funny little poem that uses just four lines. The first two lines
rhyme and the last two lines rhyme:

To my beautiful mother
you care for me and my brother
you give us hugs when we are sad
sorry if we drive you mad.

This type of poem is called a **clerihew**, and we've met it before - on page 66. (Turn back if you need a reminder!) The first line always ends with a name, so you'll need to think of some words to rhyme with this name. Below are some ideas to get you going.

Mother: brother, cover, another, other

Father: rather, lather (to make something soapy), stronger, washer

Mum: tum, hum, gum

Dad: launch pad, lad, had

Carer: sharer (someone who shares), fairer, repairer

Write your rhyming words here!

Write a clerihew for your mum, dad, carer – or anyone else who you think deserves a poem! Use some of the rhyming words from page 118. Remember that the first two lines will have one rhyme (for example mother/brother) and that the second two lines will use a different rhyme (such as tum/hum).

Halloween Poems

These are the treats I got when trick-or-treating
Jelly zombie babies
Cola blood bottles
Lolly-eye pops
These are the treats I got when trick-or-treating
Fizzy veins
Drooling gob stoppers
Brain-popping candy
These are the treats I got when trick-or-treating!

YOU ARE A POET

Imagine some scary-sounding snacks, such as: jelly zombie babies, fizzy veins, lolly-eye pops. Create a poem about spooky Halloween treats! You might want to use a repeating line like in the poem on page 121.

Christmas Poems

There are so many things to inspire a Christmas poem: presents, Christmas trees, decorations, elves, steaming Christmas dinner, Christmas pudding and of course SANTA and his sleigh. Choose your favourite thing about Christmas and write a poem about it. Copy your poem into your Christmas cards and give them to your friends and family!

YOU ARE A POET

Did you know that every single snowflake is different? Snowflakes are tiny ice crystals made in rain clouds – if you have been outside when it is snowing, you have been covered in millions of tiny snowflakes.

Imagine a snowflake is falling from the clouds. Write a poem about what it might see:

✮ Did it see the lights of a city?
✮ Did it see the stars?
✮ Did it see the moon?
✮ Did it start to melt as it fell?
✮ Did it blow on the wind?
✮ Where did it land?
✮ How did it feel?

If you'd like an extra challenge, try writing your snowflake poem in the shape of a snowflake. You could cut it out, stick a string loop to the top, and hang it up as a festive decoration!

POETRY IN SCHOOL

School is a great place to explore poetry. You can hunt for found poems along the book shelves and display boards, be inspired by assemblies, dinner queues and playtimes, and set up groups with friends where you can read and write poems together. Here are a few ways that you can have fun with poetry in your school.

Keeping A Poetry Notebook

A poetry notebook is a great place to keep your poems and to collect ideas. Your notebook could be a school exercise book (if your school has any spare), a special notebook bought from a shop, or simply some pieces of paper stapled together.

You might end up with hundreds of notebooks all filled with ideas, the beginnings of poems, the ends of poems, forgotten poems and finished poems. If you find something inspiring: a leaf, a flyer, an interesting photo or picture, stick it in your notebook.

Try to keep your notebook and a pen or pencil nearby, even when you are in bed – just in case a brilliant idea comes to you at night, so you can quickly write it down and enjoy completing it in the morning.

Poetry In The Playground

The outside is full of ideas for poems. If your school allows it, take your notebook and pen or pencil outside during break time. Find a quiet corner to sit and watch what is happening.

- ✯ What games are being played?
- ✯ What can you hear?
- ✯ What are the trees doing?
- ✯ What are your teachers doing?
- ✯ How are your classmates moving? Are they running? Jumping? Leaping?

Note down any words or phrases and remember that you do not have to write a full poem – you can just collect sights and sounds and phrases. Have fun with what you write!

You could also play these games in the playground:

What's The Word, Mr Wolf

This is like the classic game 'What's the time, Mr Wolf?', but the wolf calls out words (instead of times). You'll need at least four players.

One person is nominated to be the wolf, and they stand away from everyone else. The players opposite the wolf shout out "What's the word, Mr Wolf?"

Mr Wolf shouts out a word that is easy for everyone to spell, such as RUN, BANG, SHEEP, or any word they like. The players then spell out the word: taking a step towards the wolf on each letter. So if they were spelling out BANG they would take four steps: B – A – N – G.

The players ask the wolf "What's the word, Mr Wolf?" and the game repeats: until the wolf decides to answer with "DINNERTIME!" The wolf then chases the players back to their starting position. If any players are caught, they become the wolf.

Word Association

Words that are associated with each other connect in some way, for example: 'water' associates with 'tap', and 'sun' associates with 'moon'. For this game you will need at least four players.

Stand in a circle and choose someone to go first. They will choose a word and say what it is like (they will describe it like a simile – see page 44). For example: "A window is like an eye".

The next person to their left will start with the last word "eye" and say "an eye is like a ball". The next person to their left will start with the last word "ball" and say "a ball is like a..." and so on!

Poetry Reading Group

A poetry reading group could meet at lunch or break time, in the playground, or in the lunch hall. Ask a teacher if there is a room you can use to hold the club in, and if you have a library at your school ask your librarian (or a teacher) for some advice on poets or poetry books to read. You could each bring a poem to share to the group, or you could tell everyone to read a poem before coming to the group and then you can all talk about it.

Gather some friends who enjoy reading poems together, or make it a club for the whole school – make posters letting other students know where and when you meet. Design a poster on the next pages.

Poetry Writing Group

This could run in the same way as a poetry reading group – except you will be writing, rather than reading, poems. Use the 'You Are A Poet' challenges from this book and work individually, in pairs, or as a big group. This is a brilliant way to share your poems with each other and get feedback. Writing can be a very private activity so when sharing poems, members of the group must be kind and only give constructive feedback – and only if the poet wants it. It is far more useful for a poet to hear what someone notices about a poem or remembers rather than what is liked or disliked.

Performance Poetry Team

Why not perform poems as a group? You could perform both individual and group poems. Make some time to rehearse together during lunchtimes or breaks. When you have practiced a few times you could ask your teachers if you could do a performance in an assembly, or visit some other classes during registration to share a short poem or two.

137

Poetry Board

Does your class have a display board? Ask your teacher if you could create a Poetry Board where students can pin up their poems for others to read. The board could be as stylish or as simple as you like! You could even have a place on the board where people can leave positive comments about the poems they read.

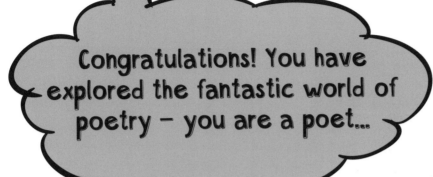

Congratulations! You have explored the fantastic world of poetry – you are a poet...

You are a poet,
you ace acrostics
ooze onomatopoeia
you twist your tongue
you take rhymes to the next tier.

You are a poet,
you dangle diagrams
with a buggy delight
you hunt for similes
and wrestle metaphors with might.

You are a poet,
you vault over verbs
you sing of the seasons
you save in a word bank and
you give the stars reason.

You are a poet,
you juggle syllables
and make colours smell
you howl haikus
and let shape poems swell.

You are a poet,
with a picture of words
you make laughter creep
and breathe life into rivers
your notebook weeps.

You are a poet
don't ever doubt
your ideas are magic
let the world hear you shout.

Scribbling Space

CONGRATULATIONS

YOU ARE
A POET

This is to certify that

....

has wrestled with metaphors,
twisted their tongue and vaulted over verbs,
and can now call themselves a poet.